HEAVENLY MATCH

Finding the Companion Jesus Has Prepared for You

J. MICHAEL LEWIS

Heavenly Match
Copyright © 2024 J. Michael Lewis

All rights reserved. No part of this book may be used or reproduced by any means, graphic, electronic, or mechanical, including photocopying, recording, taping or by any information storage retrieval system without the written permission of the author except in the case of brief quotations embodied in critical articles and reviews.

Because of the dynamic nature of the Internet, any web addresses or links contained in this book may have changed since publication and may no longer be valid. The views expressed in this work are solely those of the author and do not necessarily reflect the views of the publisher, and the publisher hereby disclaims any responsibility for them.

Paperback: 978-1-952648-87-8

CONTENTS

Acknowledgements 1
Preface 2
The Situation 6
    I Wonder What The Problems Are?
Objectives And Alternatives 12
    Do You Really Want A Mate, Or Would A Basset Hound Do?
Self Assessment 19
    Brace Yourself. Have You Taken A Long Look In A Mirror Lately? 19
Perception 29
    Beauty And Other Perceptions Are In The Eye Of The Beholder. 29
Criteria For Selection 34
    Can You Really Tell How Good A Companion Will Be
    Before The Last "I Do" Is Said And Done?
The Approach 41
    What Is Meant To Be Will Be, Especially If You Have A Good Plan
Execution 49
    Couch Potatoes And Hermits Don't Meet Many People,
    But Turtles Have A Lot Of Possibilities
Extras 56
    Pick And Choose As You Please. 56
Summary 63
    All Jokes Aside, How Well Have You Read Between The Lines? 63
Bibliography 67
About The Author 69

Acknowledgements

The impossible task of recognizing everyone who helped make this creative endeavor successful can only be approached by identifying the vital few who provided the most significant and direct contributions:

To my four special daughters, for giving me a reason to write.

To my best friend and wife, BJ, for giving me the joy of good companionship.

To my coach and confidant, Sam, for giving me encouragement, advice and perspective.

To my editor and friend, Sonya Cashdan, for giving me her open mind and open heart, for sharing her precious time and talents, for adding warmth, generosity, and humor to our work, and mostly for taking me seriously.

Any errors or omissions belong to the author.

PREFACE

God and Jesus have an influence on all of us getting married. They impact us to have marriage for our whole life. God started our marriage when time began. In the beginning God started with Adam and Eve in the Garden of Eden with lifetime love in their hearts for each other. He also did the same for Noah and his family. God gave them the ability to have children. With our children we greatly increase our world population. God and Jesus today have a strong impact on all of us by filling our hearts with love.

Solomon, in his vast wisdom, wrote of the importance of love experienced between a man and a woman in marriage. In "The Song of Songs," he vividly presents this relationship as the greatest fulfillment available in earthly life. However, some demographic experts estimate the number of single adults in the United States at nearly 90 million.

As younger Americans wait longer to marry and older Americans live longer after being widowed, the number of singles grows. Increased divorce rates and alternate lifestyles among the middle-aged also contribute to this trend. Of the 80 million Americans between the ages of 30 and 50, twenty million lack companions: single, divorced, or widowed, an alarming 25 to 50% of us are missing the best that this life has to offer. Finding a good companion ranks high among the many challenges adults face. You can face them and win if you have the desire and know-how: success depends on you. For each challenge, a "Best-Known Method" of meeting it has emerged from the experiences of others. The current proliferation of information makes these "Best-Known Methods" usually well-documented and readily available for your use.

Most of us hesitate to pursue profound knowledge because of the heavy stresses that already burden us; in a hectic life, the pressure to learn a new method can look like just one more problem. But now you have another choice: Publications for Less Stress and More Success!

This book (and others in the Paradox Series) will provide you with best-known methods for success in a form that is helpful, enjoyable, and relaxing. In general, you can apply these methods to improve your life and to ease your stress; in particular, you can use the methods which follow to locate, assess, and secure a companion. For many of us, romantic adventures repeatedly end in failure. With 10 million available candidates for companionship of each sex, why should millions of good and decent people have to go through life unpartnered? Although some, of course, are single by choice, the majority simply don't seem to know how to find a suitable and willing mate.

If you're one of that majority, mourn no more. This painful and very human problem can be approached like many others in a completely different realm: business and industry. The principles of achieving high performance and excellence in business and industry actually fit the human situation quite well. Five years of numerous practical experiments in applying best-known methods indicate that almost anyone can find a good companion. Not everyone involved in applying high-performance principles has found the right companion yet, but most of the trial group have done so, and the rest are making encouraging progress.

The following approach for finding a good companion results from extensive research on the principles and methods of dating, romance, and matchmaking, combined with some personal experience and success in this area. Here, assembled in condensed form, you will discover an effective combined approach based on the work of numerous experts. Since these best-known methods are common to numerous authors and authorities, no specific sources are cited, although a helpful list of further readings is added for the user's convenience. The successful people within the following chapters really exist, with identities altered or blended to protect their privacy; in each of their lives, something was missing: a companion. The whimsical presentation of their situations and solutions incorporates a serious intent; as you read each chapter, you may want to review the All-Serious outline in Chapter 9, provided as a reference while you read and learn. It will reinforce critical points while you apply your learning and improve your approach. Our concept is really very simple; you provide the life challenges that will provide the formula for success. So read, relax, enjoy, learn, and succeed. The life you improve may be your own!

THE SITUATION

I WONDER WHAT THE PROBLEMS ARE?

*L*et's try to understand a typical situation: Helen, the old high school chum. Cheerleader and homecoming queen, Helen, once voted "Most Likely To Succeed," now feels middle age creeping upon her. Overcome with the reality of growing old, she looks back on her life, disappointed with where she has been and what she has accomplished. Helen hasn't lived out the dream she once envisioned: she has failed to get a modeling contract; no one has named her Woman of the Year; she is not on a single "Who's Who" list. Reflecting reluctantly, Helen reviews a life not even vaguely resembling those youthful dreams. How did she ever get here? To intensify her emotional pain, her body is beginning to sag in some very inconvenient places, with wrinkles mapping out her life for all to see. Her hair has become thinner, slightly gray; for every ache and pain that aspirin relieves, two new ones surface. Slowly and inexorably getting older, Helen despairs at what she sees.

Recognize the story? Now add to this bleak situation the fact that Helen lacks a mate. Why? Maybe she just hasn't taken the time to find one. Maybe she has shopped around and found the price too high. Perhaps she's waiting for a buyers' market. She remembers poignantly the good mate of her youth whom misfortune took away and another who left for reasons unknown.

HELEN

Whatever the cause, Helen feels lonely, almost desperate for companionship. She yearns for a mate to share life's special moments, but from her perspective, all the candidates have been "picked over, culled out, damaged, dumped, and left for dead." Sound familiar? Helen's story probably strikes close enough to home to create depression, mid-life crisis, and bleeding ulcers. However, life need not remain bleak; Helen hasn't found a good companion yet, but tens of thousands in her situation have done so. Rosemary provides proof positive that the road to success is never too long.

Listen to her story: Five years ago, Rosemary's husband left her for a cute, young receptionist at his racquet club, leaving Rosey (as her close friends call her) a divorced mother of three preteen boys. A gourmet cook and manager of a successful catering service, Rosey feels both financially secure and basically content in her role as a single parent. Although she relishes the daily trips to the Little League and savors her quiet evenings at home, something is missing. Since her ex-husband has completely deserted her sons, she worries about their lacking a fatherly influence and role model. She also ponders what she will do with herself when her boys grow up and leave home. A few months ago, Rosey sought some advice from a trusted friend who knew how to apply good psychology and common sense to her dilemma. By following methods such as those presented in this book, Rosey has found a good companion; in fact, she plans to be married next June. Gaining what had been missing in her life, she feels happier than she ever thought possible. On the way to finding a mate, Rosey had to solve a couple of personal problems and develop some new attitudes; she also had to tidy up her appearance and change some unbecoming habits. Putting her past behind her, she had to look to the future. It wasn't easy, but she succeeded because she learned a good method, kept her determination, and remained optimistic that the right mate for her was out there somewhere. Rosey looked on the proverbial bright side, and you have good reason to do likewise.

ROSEY

Reach for your sun shades! People who learn from their mistakes improve as candidates for companionship the next time around. In fact, people often blossom and become far more appealing at 40 than they were at 20, developing new and more interesting personal qualities or discovering attributes that have been hidden or unappreciated. People can realize that they are not so bad as others have perceived them to be. Some people just have not met the right person to help them bloom. Most important of all, some people have not met you - and you have not met them. Don't give up on yourself until you have tried this book's approach to success. Among the "picked over, culled out, damaged, dumped, and left for dead," you could not be any worse than anyone else. The beauty of character as well as of body definitely resides in the perceptions of the beholder. As long as trial and error persist, new opportunities can come your way. As long as peace and war alternate, situations in your life can change. As long as marriage and divorce compete, new candidates are created each day. You can change your fortunes in romance, achieving less stress and more success with just a little extra knowledge and a few adjustments. It's entirely up to you.

ROSEY WITH SOME NEW ATTITUDES

OBJECTIVES AND ALTERNATIVES

DO YOU REALLY WANT A MATE, OR WOULD A BASSET HOUND DO?

*I*s there any reasonably acceptable alternative to human companionship? Studies show that the companionship of a dog creates a peaceful, calming effect, which reduces stress, lowers blood pressure, and improves one's general health. In contrast, some human companionships can produce quite the opposite effect. So, what drives someone to think that taking another person as a companion or mate provides the best answer for happiness? The old adage that "a dog is man's (or woman's) best friend" was not coined by some desperate pet owner with an unwanted litter of puppies. Perhaps single adults should be more realistic about the ever-loving, ever-present, ever-available canine, which comes fully assembled with a lifetime guarantee: it will remain absolutely free of complaints, questions, doubts, demands, and threats of divorce. No matter how much the owner ignores the dog, it always forgives and cuddles up. Of course, any pet requires food, water, and occasional medication. Fleas, ticks, foul breath, and chewed slippers cause minor problems. The question remains: do you really want a human mate? Many millions lead contented lives without one—you must honestly evaluate your objectives. Middle age brings with it an entirely different set of concerns from those of youth. Remember the Big Six objectives of teenage life? For most adolescents, the list probably read thus:

WILL A BASSET HOUND DO?

1. Freedom from Parental Control
2. Money to Spend
3. A Big Car (for guys) and A Big Wedding (for girls)
4. Sex
5. Sex
6. More Sex (Or for many girls - Romance, Romance, and More Romance).

As people approac.h middle age, they discover that their objectives are becoming quite different, broadening in both number and scope. New priorities emerge, priorities necessary to "put things in order" in the later years. Maturity usually produces more realistic objectives, probably similar to these:

1. Health, Well-Being, and Safety
2. Having Kids and Getting Them Through College
3. Protecting Personal Interests in Life (Family, Friends, Career, Business, Etc.)
4. Enriching One's Home Life and Finding Meaningful Leisure Activities
5. Long-Term Financial Security
6. Money to Spend
7. A Big Car and a Big House
8. Sex/Romance
9. Sex
10. More Sex

These points force you to ask yourself these questions: "Do I really want a mate?" and "Why?" A look at one's own objectives might suggest investigating other alternatives. Take, for example, the case of Sebastian, a lifelong bachelor and an "intellectual" type with college degrees in physics and engineering, whose self-acquired mastery of the stock market has produced a multi-million dollar bank account.

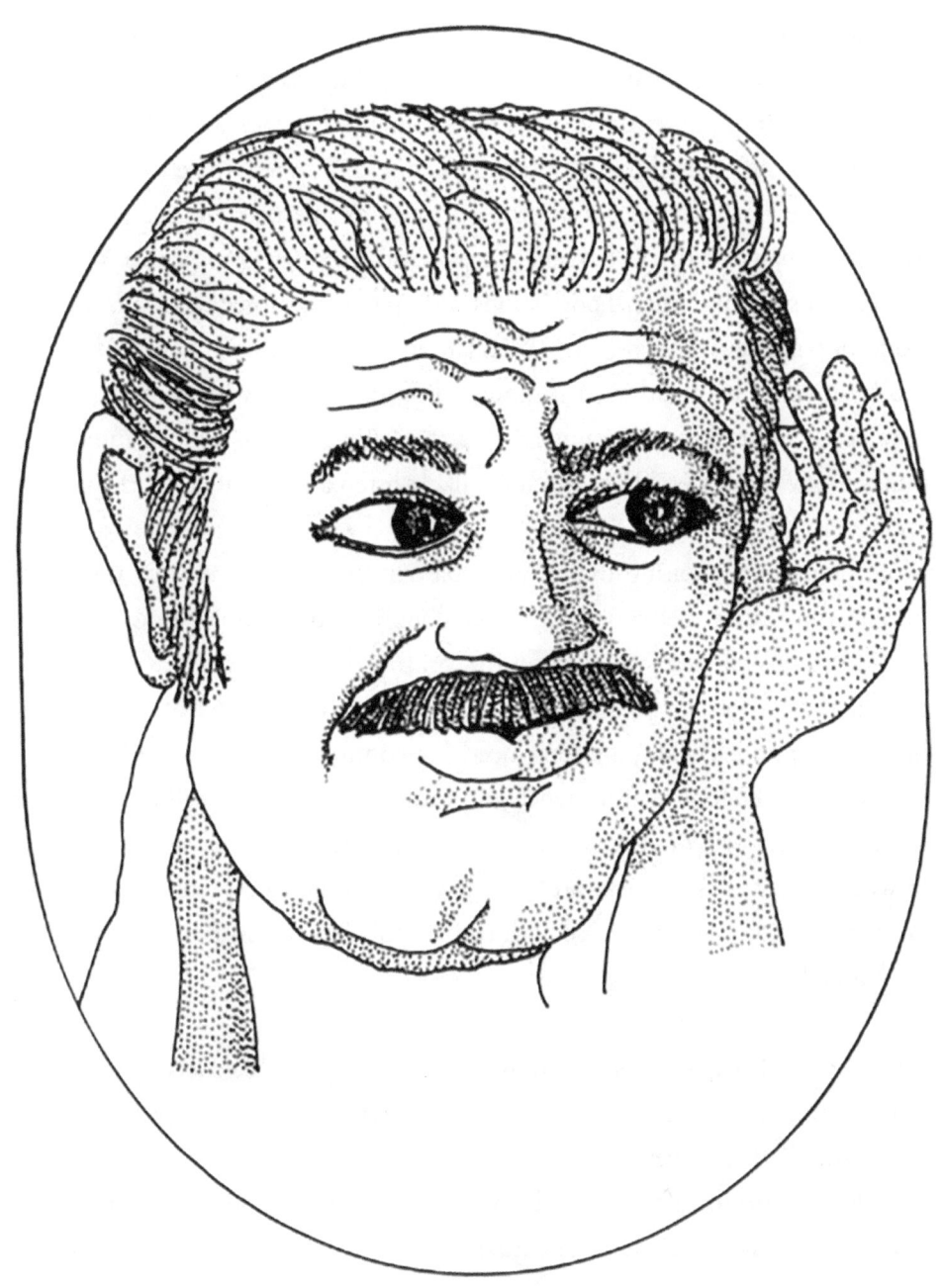

SEBASTIAN

Back in his school days, Sebastian was a ranking member of the "Campus Nerds," who never dated or showed any interest in girls. His preoccupation with accumulating financial wealth, scientific knowledge, and professional status began consuming all of his energies at age fifteen. Some thirty years later, Sebastian has indeed met the goals of his youth, but has also decided that his life lacks something; something is missing. Having discovered a need for personal intimacy, he finally understands why so many of his peers found girls more interesting than a textbook, a financial report, or a company prospectus. Without companionship, his material possessions add up to little more than a comfortable world of emptiness. Has he waited too late to start the search? Never! Although Sebastian spent his youth as a fumbling, bumbling idiot with women, he has now become successful, accomplished, and confident, with a lot of interesting things to say to women. They will most likely listen and enjoy his company.

More prepared for dating than ever, Sebastian nonetheless remains unsure of his courtship skills. Before plunging headlong into the dating game, Sebastian considered several alternatives to fill the voids in his life. Feeling a strong need to hear the "pitter-patter of little feet," he acquired two dozen baby ducks for his garden pond. Feeling a strong need for comfort, protection, and security, he installed a 12-foot security fence and acquired a pit bull. Feeling a need for someone trustworthy to discuss personal matters, he invited his mother to move in with him. Well, the ducks and the fence have produced pretty good results, but some major problems arose with the pit bull and Mom. Batting 0.500 isn't all that bad!

Sebastian wisely explored other alternatives offered by the high-tech world of the '90s: computer graphics and VCRs to stimulate his visual senses; .357 magnums and compact disc players to stimulate his auditory senses; imported foods and beverages to stimulate his palate. Finally, he even tried robotic maids and cooks to fulfill his social needs; in fact, he tried every imaginable alternative to a binding relationship with another person, but found something still missing. Nothing filled the void.

NO ARTIFICIAL SUBSTITUTE WILL DO

Sebastian realized that only a warm, breathing, loving human could meet his objectives and needs. Since "nothing ticks like a Rolex," Sebastian admitted that no substitutes would alleviate his loneliness; if your needs resemble his, no substitutes will do for you. No genuine substitute for a human companion exists—so why know your objectives and carefully consider alternatives? If nothing else, this step will prove whether you truly need "the real thing." The chances are good that you do. However, if the very real pleasures of solitude and independence do satisfy your needs, there is always the reliable basset hound.

SELF ASSESSMENT

BRACE YOURSELF. HAVE YOU TAKEN A LONG LOOK IN A MIRROR LATELY?

*U*nderstanding yourself requires doing an honest, objective self-assessment—a difficult task. Although we may have little trouble analyzing others, analyzing ourselves presents an entirely different proposition. Most of us have acquired considerable skill at looking outward into the world but often become blind to looking inward at our own person. Perhaps we even avoid looking closely into mirrors! Although our attractiveness as whole people really counts most to others, usually we see only what we want or fear to see, a clouded and fragmented image of ourselves. Knowing who we are undergirds success. To chart our destinies, we must seek answers to the elusive "What?", "Why?", "When?", and "How?" questions about our personalities, behaviors, and needs. Understanding these provides a key that opens previously unlocked doors in our lives, especially the door of human companionship.

HELEN SEES VERY LITTLE IN HER MIRROR

By now, you probably realize that Helen, whom you met a few pages ago, lacked self-awareness. She knew a few Whats and Whens about herself, and even fewer Whys and Hows. As an adolescent, Helen drove herself to garner attention, winning all the top honors in our class—she would have liked a "Here's Helen" section in the yearbook—but she didn't really perceive or understand the drive. Like many of us, she probably knew herself less than she knew almost anyone around her, seeing nothing beyond that pretty face, those classy clothes, and that nice figure in her mirror. Self-assessment, a lifelong process, teaches us more about our feelings, reactions, and needs with each new experience—and sometimes it teaches us things we'd rather not find out. Perhaps Helen never found a good companion because she never found herself, despite seeking several sorts of counseling, including a few visits to a "shrink."

Since junior high aptitude tests had proved inaccurate and useless (Helen did not want to be a flight attendant, social worker, or entomologist), Helen had her personality type assessed during one counseling session. From this assessment, she acquired the new identities of Reactor, Controller, Persistor, and Sensor, which seemed to provide her more limitations than opportunities for growth. Dozens of those "How Good a Whatever Are You?" quizzes in the women's magazines always provide only an average score. She even studies the Zodiac Signs, sometimes predicting how she might feel on a given day. In desperation to learn who she really is, Helen has even contemplated visiting a palmist or buying one of those numerology profiles she's seen advertised. However, with all that background information, she still may be the last to know anything about her real, inward self.

Does Helen know herself well enough to find a good companion? Her name, address, social security number, credit cards, and driver's license reveal only her assigned statistics. But who is she really? What are her general strengths and weaknesses? Does she have any particular capabilities? Does she possess any special knowledge, skills, or personal qualities? Does she have any major shortcomings, handicaps, or disabilities? Does she have any significant habits, either good or bad? Does she have any strong preferences, hobbies, commitments, aversions, fixations, or obsessions? Does she have a vocation? Does she radiate confidence and believe in her own competence? What attributes does she bring to the arena of loving relationships?

What is Helen's personal makeup? What emotions can she experience? Is she nervous and oversensitive or always calm, collected, and impervious to emotional stimuli? Is she more of an optimist, a pessimist, or an "apathist"? Is she light-hearted or does she take herself too seriously? Are her spirits usually high or low? Is she easily discouraged or disappointed? Is she a griper, a whiner, a growler, or a gnawer? Is she a quitter with the determination of fluff or a survivor with the determination of steel?

What physical characteristics does Helen project? Firm or soft, plump or thin, fit or unhealthy? What impression do her clothes make? What image do her hairstyle, makeup, jewelry, and even her car present? Does she have "sex appeal"? How does she smell: delicious, worldly, pleasant, clean, or otherwise? What overall appearance do her collective features create: a stunningly well-assembled package of dazzling delights; a pleasingly average, full assortment of sweets and sours; or a wildly concocted assemblage of uniquely interesting surprises?

How well does Helen communicate? Can she express her thoughts and feelings accurately and rationally? Does she display tact and poise in conversation? Is she comfortable talking in front of or among a group? Can she listen well, or does she chatter nervously without purpose even when her brain is not "in gear"?

What are Helen's primary values and their origins? What criteria does she use to make decisions and set priorities? What does she stand for? Against? What is important to her: Peace? Friendship? Truth? Knowledge? Wisdom? Freedom? Health? Equality? Happiness? Is she honest and responsible? Does she believe in fair play, the Good Life, the Golden Rule, the Honor Code, and "life, liberty, and the pursuit of happiness"? Does she live by the Girl Scout Motto and think we should retire the national debt?

How does Helen feel about herself? Does she possess a positive self-concept, a high self-worth? Does she feel special? Does she like herself? Does she feel okay? Is she her own best friend or her own worst enemy? Does she have a good time alone?

How does Helen relate to others? Does she generally prefer companionship or solitude? Does she trust other people, expecting the best from them, or does she generally expect to be cheated, stepped on, and hurt? And what do other people really think of her? Do they normally like her? Does she get invited to many parties? In a crowd, does she stand out, or do people even notice her presence? Does she attract people, or do they avoid her company? Does she have any best friends? Has anyone ever proposed marriage to her? Has anyone asked her out on a date recently? If she were someone else, would she go out with herself?

Self-assessment even includes how children and animals respond to her. Do infants always cry and spit up when she holds them, or do they gurgle and coo? How many dogs have ever threatened or bitten her? Do cats immediately pronounce her lap acceptable? Do flowers wilt when she appears?

What is Helen's concept of friendship and love? During childhood, did she know with confidence that her mother and father loved her? Did she feel that her parents' love would always be available to her regardless of what she said, how she looked, or what she did? Did other children willingly play with her, or did her mother have to coax and bribe them with candy and other treats? Does she know the true meaning of unconditional love? Does she view friendship and love as primarily giving or primarily taking?

I certainly don't know, and right now Helen doesn't, either. She needs to take a long look into a mirror, or literally make some lists, and honestly assess herself.

Lilly, on the other hand, provides an excellent example of self-awareness. She has taken a close look both into a mirror and into her mind, learning a lot of valuable things about herself and thus starting on the road to finding a good companion. A registered nurse and a single parent to a 20-year-old college coed, Lilly lost her husband to a fatal heart attack while he was jogging several years ago. Almost a fanatic about fitness and health, Lilly keeps herself trim and firm, enjoying a comfortable existence in a stylish condominium. Devastated by the loss of her husband, at first, Lilly could not even think about finding a new companion. Now she has an occasional short and somewhat satisfying romantic fling, but something is always missing: she longs for a permanent relationship with a man who will appreciate her dedicated affections. While Lilly needs a man with a gentle touch who will allow her to smother him with admiring devotion, somehow her men always get scared and run off in a panic; until recently she didn't understand Why and How she was causing that reaction.

With the help of her friends, Lilly began an honest evaluation of herself: she examined her habits and tendencies, began to understand her feelings, read books on self-analysis and self-worth. As she listened to her trusted friends and to herself, she learned to understand her Whats and Whys and Whens and Hows. When Lilly finally found herself, she realized why she couldn't find a permanent mate. With some new self-awareness, she has gained new hope for success.

LILY

Lilly's self-awareness received an additional boost one evening while she conversed with a new lover. After a romantic interlude, her friend related an amazing discovery he had made about himself: while visiting his counselor, he was recalling his childhood and recounting the shortcomings of his father. The counselor interrupted his story with a stunning observation: "You know, you may be more like your dad than you would like to admit." With no time to brace himself, Lilly's lover had at first resisted the idea, but ever since then he has noticed similarities unrecognized before. Developing a much deeper insight into himself, he has become much more accepting and much less critical of his dad. Since then he has hardly slept a wink from the shock of it all. Not long after that romantic evening, Lilly received a surprise package in the mail from her mother. The package contained a coffee mug with the inscription, "Congratulate me! I have officially become my mother."

Lilly too has come to a startling realization: studying someone like yourself can often be a lot easier than studying yourself. Look closely at your parents, siblings, childhood friends, and professional peers. The benefits may be invaluable.

LILLY STUDIES MOM

The successes and failures of Lilly and Helen offer a clear message: forget the astrologer, the palmist, and the numerologist, and ask your mirror and your memories instead. You can see in them what the future holds for your finding a good companion. Try to see yourself as others do, and then make some changes that will make you more attractive to them. Your mirror is the only consultant you need.

PERCEPTION

BEAUTY AND OTHER PERCEPTIONS ARE IN THE EYE OF THE BEHOLDER.

A couple of years ago at a family gathering, I got reacquainted with Walter, a distant cousin whom I remembered as handsome, good-natured, well-mannered, and athletic. Very successful with the ladies and an accomplished salesman by trade, Walter always commanded attention and drew people to him. Although I once perceived Walter as described above, twenty years later I could hardly recognize him. A shadow of the person I had once known, no longer the pride of the family, he was sitting alone when I first noticed him. Worn and defeated, overweight, poorly groomed, and poorly dressed, Walter now chain-smoked and appeared to have lost most of his once unbreakable self-confidence. Looking almost like a lost clown from the circus, he seemed somewhat embarrassed to meet me again; the resulting impression failed to evoke my compassion.

From the family grapevine, I knew that Walter had failed at marriage three times and had changed jobs at least two dozen times in the past twenty years. Furthermore, he had avoided contact with family members for several years, but I had no idea how far he had allowed himself to fall from respectability. Although I had once perceived him as a winning entry in any race, now I feared that he would be lucky to finish last. Had Walter really changed? Were my perceptions of him becoming a loser valid? Or were my original perceptions wrong? To my amazement, Walter confided that he was seeking a new companion and asked if I knew of any candidates. Shocked at his appearance and dumbfounded at what I was hearing, I could find no words of encouragement for him.

What I failed to realize at that family gathering was that Walter had not lost his self-awareness or his skills of salesmanship. He had, in fact, identified things about himself that he wanted to change because he knew the realities of perception, having long ago accepted the fact that perception equals reality to the beholder. For Walter, as for most people, no lasting, painful changes would be necessary if he could achieve a different presentation of his assets.

Let's think about the potential that perception still has for anyone seeking a companion. Perception cannot always be pinpointed and explained. For instance, how many absolute values exist in the world? How many things can really be precisely defined in unquestionable, specific, quantitative terms?

Consider for a moment the perceptions we develop of other people by reacting to their physical characteristics. Most of us accept that "beauty is in the eye of the beholder," but what exactly is "ugly"? At what point, for example, does one's breath become offensive enough to qualify as "bad"—what fine line divides pleasing fragrance from odor? What determines the cutoff points between skinny and slender, pleasingly plump and obese? Where does boring end and stimulating begin? What is appealing and sexy and what is not? Who decides whether or not Walter equals a good candidate for marriage? While he knew that he was not creating a positive impression, he also knew that beauty and perception reside in the eye of the beholder; nobody can confidently define romantic attractiveness and how to get it. Walter could make himself interesting, fun-loving, pleasant, healthy, energetic, and enthusiastic about life again. Beyond these appearances, he need not worry about anything as uncontrollable as sex appeal.

WALTER
(NOT THE PERSON I ONCE KNEW)

Because of our preconceptions, perception means everything. Ask anyone if men who wear white T-shirts with rolled-up sleeves and ride motorcycles are "hoods"? If women who wear pink body stockings and bright lipstick are "on the make"? If men who wear earrings and carry purses are effeminate? If someone who buys groceries with food stamps is a "lazy free-loader"? If all blonde women who chew gum in public are brainless? Perception is everything. Look into the mirror again: what perceptions do you create for those you know and meet with your perfume or aftershave, breath, eye contact, and smile? What message do you convey with your hair, eyes, nails, complexion, and posture? With your clothes, car, friends, home, and career?

To succeed in your quest for a companion, you must first accept the preeminence of perception and then consciously adjust the way others perceive you. Your heart and brain may be saying "yes" to a potential mate, but those stains on your shirt may be saying "No, No, No!" That gold front tooth which drew admiring eyes in high school now draws glances of dismay. That "Make Love, Not War" lapel button you have cherished since college may project a message besides that of the words themselves. Perception is everything. It may be time to start that exercise program, get that hair trimmed and re-styled, or even get that nose straightened. It may be time to stick to that diet, take up an active hobby, or even get that second chin lifted. It may be time to replace that too-youthful or too-sensible wardrobe or even to get a few months of counseling for that shyness or lack of self-confidence.

With some sincere **attention to important details** and some minor corrective actions, Walter recreated the appearance of the dashing gentleman he once was. With several seriously interested female companions, he will soon find—and this time keep—wife number four. Like Walter, you can become almost anything you want. You are restricted only by your budget, your comfort zone, your self-discipline, and perhaps your pain threshold. Just be careful not to change too much; you undoubtedly have many qualities well worth keeping just as they are.

**WALTER
(JUST A LITTLE MORE ATTENTION TO DETAIL)**

CRITERIA FOR SELECTION

CAN YOU REALLY TELL HOW GOOD A COMPANION WILL BE BEFORE THE LAST "I DO" IS SAID AND DONE?

Everyone holds different ideas about what makes a good mate. Some people expect more than others, being more critical in their judgments, more demanding in their expectations, and less tolerant of failures. Some people possess more independence, emotional security, and self-reliance. Some have more likes and dislikes; others simply have more needs. The important question is this: What is important to you? What criteria will you use to select Mr. or Ms. Right? You would probably sacrifice a lot to find someone with the following characteristics:

1. Physical attractiveness
2. Sensitivity to and respect for your dignity and self-worth
3. A sense of humor
4. Good listening skills

5. Tolerance for your weaknesses, opposite points of view, and religious preferences
6. Sexual compatibility
7. Willingness to share household chores
8. Honesty, reliability, and trustworthiness
9. Acceptance of your family and friends
10. Security enough to allow you freedom to be yourself

Although the list contains few items, no reasonable person can expect to find anyone with all of these assets. Because these ten requirements form the inflexible expectations that Hilda, my financial advisor, insists upon for her potential companions, all she has found thus far is disappointment in her life.

To Hilda, CPA means both Certified Public Accountant and "Certified People Assessor." Although she has never taken a chance on marriage, she considers herself an authority on the subject, forever analyzing people around her, especially the "undeserving," "ungrateful," "crude" males. She constantly offers advice on marital and related social problems. Hilda's perfectionism and meticulous attention to detail manifest themselves in her neat appearance, proper behavior, and "pure" lifestyle. She avidly follows professional sports, preferring them because they display a discipline, order, and excellence rarely present in everyday life. Craving a mate, she nonetheless holds out for a Mr. Right who fully satisfies the ten characteristics listed above—and MORE.

Hilda expects far too much; her Mr. Right probably does not exist. Even if he does, how could anyone possibly be happy with someone so reliable, predictable, and considerate? Life can sometimes be boring enough without being tied down with a "perfect" mate.

Hilda needs to reduce her list to those critical few requirements which mean the most to her. Although wisdom suggests evaluating potential mates on the basis of their readiness, willingness, and ability to fulfill all ten of her chosen qualities, it does not make sense to eliminate anyone who doesn't score a perfect TEN. Five or six strengths should meet anyone's needs, with the other four or five weaknesses providing variety and entertainment. Only in fairy tales do perfect relationships occur. Good marriages are not built with partners of perfect quality, but with patience, understanding, flexibility, and acceptance. Partners cannot consistently contribute to a relationship on a 50-50 basis, despite the scenarios on "Ozzie and Harriet" or "The Cosby Show." Reality means that knights on white horses cannot compete with sports cars on freeways, and castles harbor an abundance of mice, mold, and mildew. Reality means that you probably will not be rescued by a companion possessing all the characteristics for a lasting love relationship.

So how many of these ten should you shoot for? Are three or four out of ten good enough? That's for you to decide. But if you really want a mate, you would be wise to try for no more than four or five. Besides, how well would you score against the list yourself? Do you judge character accurately? How well can you really assess these qualities in a person before marriage?

Why not start with Hilda's ten criteria, subtracting and adding to the list based on your own preferences? Remember, though, the longer your list, the fewer candidates you will have to consider. You don't want to make it too easy for potential candidates to win your heart, but neither do you want to make it too difficult.

What happened to Hilda? She finally realized that her plans would not work and began to exercise better judgment. Yes, she had everything in her life planned and ordered just as she liked it, but life lacked something;

something was missing. After realizing that few men could or would be as neat, reliable, considerate, and productive as she wished, she learned the simple method of asking herself WHY several times to be certain her criteria merited keeping.

For example, she asked WHY it seemed so important that her mate not insist on displaying his prized collection of risque magazines on the coffee table. Hilda's answer: "My friends will likely see them." WHY is this important? Hilda's answer: "They will think he is a sick, perverted animal." WHY is this so important? Hilda's answer: "They will conclude that I am a sick, perverted animal." WHY is this important? Hilda's answer: "They may tell my mother I am a sick, perverted animal." WHY is this important? Hilda's answer: "It will hurt Mother's feelings." Stop!

Did Hilda find she had a good reason? No, so she threw the criterion out. Conversely, if she had discovered that his collection was so large that it left no room for her extensive collection of antique doorknobs, then she might have had sufficient reason to retain this criterion on her list.

Before she started asking WHY, Hilda could find a "good" reason for anything: that her companion be at least 6 feet tall and weigh no less than 185 pounds; that he not retain morning breath all day; that he be married no more than once before. She thought it important that he not toss his soiled boxers under the bed; that his best friend not be named Bubba; that he not smoke cheap cigars in the car. She even insisted that a potential mate not watch pro wrestling on TV, not sell vacuum cleaners door-to-door, and not scratch just anywhere that itches.

She soon concluded that she must have been looking for a prince. A good companion could lack all the qualities above and still be perfectly able to drag a garbage can down to the street, leave on time for work each morning, help her with the yard work, cuddle on the sofa, and tell the difference between a claw hammer and a tire tool.

HILDA ASSESES A CANDIDATE

(FROM A SAFE DISTANCE)

Like Hilda, Sebastian, whom you met earlier, began his quest with equally unrealistic expectations. He felt it really important that his companion not carry excess poundage, not have PMS more than a few days per month, and not resent having his dog in the house. He once considered it vital that she prepare several home-cooked meals each week, not have false teeth, and not enjoy RAP music. He wanted her to prefer his favorite perfume, dress in high fashion, and enjoy his favorite sport, ice hockey.

Sebastian, too, quickly concluded that he must have been looking for a princess. Even without the "musts" above, his woman still should be perfectly able to keep a comfortable home, share his joint bank account, help get the children off to school, cuddle on the sofa, hire a cleaning lady, microwave a chicken pot pie, serve his favorite cold cereal for breakfast, and realize when she has a flat tire.

The point is that you cannot have it all. After Hilda and Sebastian finally condensed their criteria lists to only three MUSTS and three more MUST NOTS, they immediately began to find good candidates for companionship, and within 18 months they both were engaged to be married. So keep your list of criteria short—and count your blessings when your companion turns out to be exactly what you had thought.

THE APPROACH

WHAT IS MEANT TO BE WILL BE, ESPECIALLY IF YOU HAVE A GOOD PLAN.

Henry, a dear friend of our household, has braved the proverbial rain, sleet, snow, and hail, as well as the attacks of our pet dachshund, each weekday for the past ten years. He delights our children with cards, letters, and packages from their grandparents; excites my wife with magazines, sweepstakes entries, and innumerable catalogs; and especially inspires me to stay productive with bills from the world's best credit card centers. Without fail, he arrives each day at 1:00 p.m. bearing a warm smile, offering a kind word, and delivering his packages of inspiration. Our family thinks Henry would make a great husband and father, but to our disappointment, he remains alone and single, a series of family misfortunes having prevented him from leaving home and getting married. Twenty years after high school, Henry spends his days performing his job, caring for his parents, and vegetating in front of the television.

For many years, Henry lived far removed from the dating world, never seeking a companion. Lately, however, he has been frequently pursued by curious companion seekers. In fact, three or four women have shown interest in him recently, but each has fled after seeing his almost fanatically faithful devotion to his parents. Until now, Henry felt fairly contented and comfortable with his life, but lately, something seems to be missing: What would it be like to have a wife, children, and a home of his own? To make his own decisions and control his own destiny? Everyone deserves a chance to realize such dreams; Henry wants a willing woman to share the adventure.

One evening last summer, on his way to buy a bag of groceries, Henry found the answer to making his dreams come true when he met an unfamiliar old man. The harmless-looking stranger obviously had many more problems than solutions; ragged and unshaven, he hesitantly held out his hand as Henry passed by. When Henry stopped, the old man asked if he could spare some money for a cup of coffee. Reminded somehow of his own father, Henry obliged with his spare change and then offered a few extra bucks for a sandwich. Delighted, the old man trembled, shook Henry's hand, smiled warmly, stammered his thanks, and asked where Henry was going. "To the grocery store," Henry replied. Still trembling, the old man observed: "I'm glad you know where you are going, because if you didn't, you might end up somewhere else."

Henry politely agreed, chuckled, and continued hastily on his way. On his trip back home, however, the man's words kept swirling in Henry's mind. The stranger had shared with him some real insight, even if expressed in a strange way: to accomplish great things in life, we have to know where we are going. We must not only dream but also plan, act, and believe, preparing ourselves for the opportunities we seek. Only then can we expect to "get lucky." If we really know where we are going, we will either find the means to achieve our objectives or create those means ourselves.

HENRY

Like Henry, everyone has dreams, fancies, visions—and occasionally nightmares. Although dreams may be vivid, dreamers often fail to reach their goals because they lack a good plan of action or cannot carry out the plan they do have. Like running a successful business, finding a good companion requires a good marketing strategy. In business, if you have a good product, you must get it to market and in front of the customer; a product stalled in the warehouse has no chance of being sold.

Finding a good companion follows a similar principle. After that enlightening trip to the grocery, Henry, deciding he needed a plan to give his dream a better chance, developed an approach for finding a mate. Had he written it down, it would have included these steps:

1. Identify places and situations where he could meet plenty of potential companions.
2. Get himself there at the right time and make contact.
3. Get their attention and present his best side.
4. Look over the candidates and decide whether he noticed any potential "winners."
5. Begin to establish relationships with those potential winners.
6. Continue to present his own wares to them while learning their strong points.
7. When convinced that he had a good candidate, he would grab her and not let go.

After reviewing his plan, Henry observed that finding a companion was a lot like fishing: whenever he failed to cast into the right stream with the right bait at the right time, he returned home empty-handed. The simple lessons he learned fishing with his Dad provided Henry some valuable clues to success. Dad taught him to identify the type of fish he wanted, secure the right equipment and bait, and pick a stream where plenty of fish were likely to be. Once there, said Dad, you pick a time when they usually bite, bait a hook, cast your line into the water, and wait for a nibble. When one strikes your line, you set the hook, reel it in, and see what you caught. If it looks good, you keep it and put it in your creel. If you realize it's not "a keeper," you toss it back without hurting it and cast your line again.

From his fishing experience, Henry also realized that opportunities to follow this approach would not present themselves without effort on his part. Unplanned "fishing trips" seldom happen. To improve his chances of success, he would need to **plan, prepare, act, and make opportunities** for himself. He joined clubs, became active in volunteer organizations, and enrolled in evening classes to get away from his parents and meet more people his own age. After asking his friends and family about their single friends, he followed up to check them out. Besides attending church functions, he began looking more closely at people around him where he shopped and worked.

Excited about his plan and determined to make it work, he learned to create even more opportunities to meet potential candidates: he advertised himself in the classified section of the newspaper, began visiting the most popular laundromats to wash his clothes, and even took a second job at a busy gas station. He made a habit of accompanying friends to their doctors' offices and other professional waiting rooms just to see who was there. He loaded his calendar with activities that put him in contact with lots of other adults: concerts, picnics, weddings, festivals, sports events, parties, dances. He knew his plan's success depended upon his meeting lots of new people, but it also depended on perception (covered in Chapter 4). Getting to the right place at the right time was important, but presenting the right image was critical, requiring careful consideration and planning.

The primary consideration here is whether to use the Perception lure (what other people think about you on their own, either rightly or wrongly) or the Deception lure (what you want them to think you are, but may not be).

When Perception doesn't produce the desired results, many people discard it and go straight to Deception, a powerful but dangerous weapon. Some rely on Deception so much that it leads to an undesirable Perception later on. Henry had enough assets without relying on deception; undoubtedly you do, too. Success for him meant changing the town's perception that he was hopelessly committed to his parents: everyone perceived that he had little time and room in his life for a companion. Henry changed this image first by letting his parents do more things for themselves, then by asking for help from others in the family and neighborhood, and finally by hiring a part-time nurse. Then, following the approach in his plan, he became active away from his home, demonstrating independence and social interest. His plan soon began to work, and within two years Henry grabbed a "keeper." Now he and his wife live in his parents' home, which Henry has converted into a private duplex. Henry and his new wife are happy, and so are Mom and Dad.

Although Henry's success warms the heart, his plan succeeded only when he tackled the two most self-defeating barriers to success, FEAR and PRIDE. At first Henry feared the simple things necessary for success, such as making eye contact. He frequently felt too proud or shy to initiate a conversation with an attractive female. However, he soon learned that middle age dating has no place for someone who cannot go up to total strangers, ask a relevant question ("Could you tell me the time?" "Which bus stops here?" "May I buy you a drink?" "May I have this dance?" "Don't you love this music?"), and smile with innocent delight when they turn around. He sometimes had to ignore his initial discomfort to get attention and create a dialogue; if he allowed fear and pride to control him, he would never find his dream.

STUCK WITHOUT A FLAN

Henry's tactics may sound far-fetched, but they worked for him. He developed a healthy philosophy about them: he could be subtle ("Did you drop this dollar bill?") or be bold ("Don't you agree that we should start recycling shampoo, shaving cream, and toothpaste?"). Whatever worked to get people's positive attention so Henry could introduce himself, he did it.

To get started in your own search for a mate, you will need a well-conceived approach. If you don't have a better one, use Henry's. Practice your techniques at home in front of a mirror or practice conversation-starters with a good friend. Mirrors and good friends don't lie, and yours will tell you when you are ready to put your techniques to work. Just keep in mind that the dating arena has no place for fear and pride, and there is no better way to get lucky than to have a good plan. Commit yourself to fishing often, staying away from dry streams, and always carrying plenty of hooks, lines, and sinkers.

EXECUTION

COUCH POTATOES AND HERMITS DON'T MEET MANY PEOPLE, BUT TURTLES HAVE A LOT OF POSSIBILITIES.

Successful people detest two situations: having no movement and having to move without direction. No movement gets you nowhere. Movement without direction gets you somewhere you might not want to be. With the ideas in Chapter 6, you can develop a plan for movement and a way to avoid these fates. To move toward success in finding a mate all you need to know is EXECUTE, EXECUTE, EXECUTE.

If you have carefully conceived your approach, it will include your best-known methods, it will feel comfortable, and it will work for you. It will also be flexible, allowing you to continually improve your methods as you execute and discover new and better ones. Maybe you still feel somewhat unsure, but that's okay too. Rosey, Sebastian, Lilly, Hilda, Walter, and Henry all had doubts at first. They all made mistakes, learned from them, and continually improved their methods to make them better.

So what are you waiting for, the next appearance of Haley's Comet? As the old saying goes, "it's time to do something, even if it's wrong." So your plan's not perfect? So not every potential companion has been warned that you are officially on the move? So you are armed with new, untested weapons? So your plan is not notarized? Big deal! Get out there and start executing!

But first, here's one key tip for that winning edge, courtesy of Curtis, a fellow Kiwanian and golf partner: while executing your plan, you should make like the ever-loving turtle. Yes, the turtle.

Curtis, a divorced father of three children in high school and college, owns and operates a small chain of convenience stores. His attractive ex-wife of 22 years left town three years ago with a younger, more interested man. An avid golfer, Curtis hardly notices the loss of his spouse. His free time after business and sports is now totally consumed by cleaning up after those three children. He manages to squeeze in an occasional date, but romance has not been high on his priority list for twenty years.

Although his life pretty much suits his liking, even Curtis notices that something is missing. He doesn't particularly want to be both father and mother, and eventually grandfather and grandmother, for the rest of his life. He would like a female companion to assume half of the parenting roles he now fulfills. Can you blame him?

When Curtis began looking for a new spouse, he established a list of criteria, did a thorough self-assessment, and developed a plan using his best-known methods. Within a year and a half, Curtis had a new partner in parenthood, grandparenthood, and golf. He swears on a stack of Golf Digests that his success was not due so much to his criteria list, his self-assessment, and his plan, as to his executing like a **turtle.**

CURTIS

Curtis means what he says. For scientific proof, he suggests seeking your advice on romance from a scientist, but for profound knowledge that only the Champions of Champions possess, he offers these stories about four successful turtles. Curtis shared them with me on the back nine on one windy, rainy Sunday morning.

Story No. 1, The Tortoise and the Hare.
Yes, I had heard this one a hundred times before, but I must not have listened well enough. The turtle beat the rabbit in a long-distance race because the turtle was more determined, more steady and sure, more disciplined, and quietly confident, unrelenting in executing his plan. On the other hand, the much faster and more confident rabbit was attracted to big snacks, long naps, foolish diversions, and various other couch potato games.

Curtis' Moral: Bunnies may be fast, have cute ears, and possess attractive tails, but often they are foolishly caught napping during competition and beaten by disciplined turtles. Be disciplined like the Turtle!

Story No. 2, The Terrapin and the Fence Post
A farmer, hosting an old friend from a big city, showed his visitor around the farm. As they stopped by a cornfield for a rest, chatting about the current price of corn, the visitor observed a Terrapin resting on top of a fence post. He remarked in fascination, "Well, look at that! I didn't know turtles could climb." The farmer smiled and explained with practical insight, "You would be surprised at what a turtle can do if given a little help."

Curtis' Moral: Climbing fence posts is not dishonorable work, and if you need the aid of a farmer to get on top of your plan, ask for help. Furthermore, if someone offers help, don't ever refuse it; turtles can even fly with a little help from others. Accept help like the Turtle!

CURTIS EXECUTING LIKE A TURTLE

Story No. 3, The Turtle and His Shell.

Turtles, surprisingly smart, know that being a couch potato or a recluse works against meeting people. So what do they do? They take their home with them while executing their plan. One such turtle on his way to his favorite melon patch met up with a hungry fox. The turtle was set on having melon for lunch; the fox had a craving for turtle soup. When the fox began a series of repeated attacks on the turtle, he simply retreated into his shell for protection. No matter how much the fox scratched, growled, bit, and kicked, he could neither penetrate the turtle's shell nor entice him to come out and fight. Each time the fox backed off, the turtle would methodically continue on toward the melon patch until the next attack. Finally, in frustration and utter defeat, the fox gave up and the turtle got his melon.

Curtis' Moral: Melon patches are full of intelligent, even-tempered, determined turtles, but rarely do you see a wild, quick-tempered fox eating turtle soup. Be determined like the Turtle!

Story No. 4, The Turtle and His Sex

For centuries, humans had been baffled with the task of determining the sex of turtles. Countless scientific studies had endeavored to unlock this elusive mystery, but repeated efforts failed to disclose answers about the distinction. Did the secret lie in the color of the head, the length of the tail, the shape of the shell, or between the legs? No one had the slightest clue.

Finally, after observing the fruitless work of a team of zoologists, a sympathetic turtle raised his weary head and cried, "If you don't know where to look, stupid, maybe you should ask one of us turtles." The turtle began to explain that sex for turtles may be difficult, but it is meaningful and much more than a visual experience. Turtles, he added, use all of their senses in sex; in fact, this command of their senses in all aspects of life has allowed them to survive for millions of years. Turtles delight in colors, aromas, tastes, and smells. Finally, he revealed that if the befuddled zoologists would clean the wax from their ears and listen, they would find the answer to their mystery. EUREKA! It was soon discovered that female turtles make a hissing sound, while male turtles grunt.

Curtis' Moral: Turtles use all of their senses while looking for the right companion, and their method of communicating with one another resembles that of humans. Listen like the turtle!

By the time we reached the eighteenth hole, I was thoroughly convinced of two things: turtles know how to execute their plans, and Curtis knows how to play golf. I took home his four turtle stories, and he took home my $25 in lost bets.

EXTRAS

PICK AND CHOOSE AS YOU PLEASE.

Even when surrounded by an active, exciting world, when one lacks a companion, something is missing. Feeling "alone in the crowd" can be an unhealthy but common situation for many single adults. In the previous chapters, we have reviewed some best-known methods for solving this problem by finding a good companion. In case you still have a question or two, consider these extra tips—you can take 'em or leave 'em. And for each of the ten tips you have here, be sure to be close to Jesus to help you succeed.

1. Be Optimistic

Recognize your limitations, but have faith and remain as optimistic as possible. To maintain objectivity about yourself, try this old Chinese proverb: "If one person tells you that you have donkey ears, take no notice; if two tell you, get yourself a saddle."

2. Be Active

Even if no one in the current field of candidates fully meets your requirements, you should be active in a relationship with the best one available. (In the world of television viewing, this strategy is called LOP, Least Objectionable Programming.) Activity keeps you fresh and sharp; inactivity breeds laziness and stagnation. To paraphrase an old song, if you can't be with the one you want, want the one you're with... until someone better comes along.

LONE IN THE CROWD

3. Be in Control

Crying and throwing tantrums may work in some situations, but only when you know exactly what you are doing. When the tantrums occur for real, you may be in trouble. Don't hurry, don't let your emotions run away with you, and don't lose control, except of course for a calculated reason—and if you've calculated the reason, you haven't lost control. Be patient, stay calm, and maintain your composure so you can execute according to plan. A loose cannon on a deck often goes overboard when the seas get rough.

4. Maintain your health, dignity, and self-respect

If you don't love and respect yourself, others probably won't either. Good health, vigor, and a well-kept body say, "I am important to ME!" Don't ever jeopardize your health for anything or anyone; once it's gone, it usually stays gone. Apply the same rule in regard to your dignity and self-respect: they can be restored only with great difficulty. Shun demeaning tactics such as whining, begging, and threatening suicide to get your way. Clinging to someone can drive him or her away from you; however, providing space and demonstrating a willingness to let go will often draw a potential mate closer to you. Remember the famous words of Cowboy Jack, "When you've got a spooked horse by the hind legs and he is trying to run away, it is best to let him run. Who knows, he may turn around and come right back."

5. Beware of Sex

Some say don't use it, some say use it prudently, and some say don't worry about it at all. I say only to beware. If you participate and the fireworks threaten your sanity, then what do you know? If you participate and don't lose your sanity, then what do you do? If you don't participate, then what do you know and what do you do? Nothing in all cases, so beware. Sexual relations rank as a leading source of pleasure, entertainment, and adventure for many couples during courtship. Responsible adults take the necessary precautions during their participation to prevent the associated physical health hazards well-known to all of us. Unfortunately, possessing far less knowledge of the associated emotional and mental hazards, we have far fewer protective devices at our disposal to combat them.

Sexual relations with a potential mate may create a strong but temporary bond or infatuation. If the sex proves satisfying, that obscures one's judgment and ability to make good assessments of the partner's potential for a lasting love relationship. Likewise, sexual relations that prove dissatisfying may produce embarrassment, disappointment, and prejudice that also interfere with one's ability to accurately assess the real value of a potential mate. Furthermore, sexual performance after marriage doesn't always resemble that experienced while dating. On the other hand, what will you know about the important issue of sexual compatibility if you don't take these warnings under advisement and test the waters anyway?

No one has the answers that are best for you; sexual participation during your assessment of potential mates should remain a personal choice for you and your plan for success. However, wisdom suggests that you treat any observed results from sexual activity with great caution, not using them to assess criteria on your MUST and WANT lists (other than for those related to sexual compatibility). Some good guidelines to follow:

(a) If you participate in sexual activities and the results turn out too good, beware of temporary insanity and focus your attention on your other criteria for a good companion.

(b) If you participate and the results turn out too bad, don't automatically declare a mismatch. Instead beware of harsh judgments and assess more thoroughly while maintaining an open mind.

(c) If you participate and the results turn out just okay, beware of future changes and continue to objectively assess your other criteria for companionship.

(d) If you don't participate, beware of the unknown and make sure enough strengths in other areas exist to compensate for whatever surprises may present themselves later.

6. Learn From Your Mistakes

The only ways to avoid mistakes are to procrastinate indefinitely, to attempt nothing new or challenging, and to take so many precautions that you can't possibly do anything. Since mistakes are inevitable, try to keep them to a minimum, viewing them as opportunities to learn and to improve. Be ready to err, but you don't have to admit those errors to anyone other than yourself.

7. Beware of Kids

If you already have kids, make sure your potential mate is allowed to succeed with them. If the potential mate has kids of his/her own, beware: they can rip your heart out and stomp it into the ground right before your eyes. If you fail to make sure that you and/or your companion succeed with each other's little darlings, they may quickly turn into little monsters who can torture an unwelcome, invading man or woman in ways beyond your imagination. They can suddenly become masters at pulling off pranks, executing practical jokes, and inflicting pain. They can instill fear that will propel a would-be companion on a one-way trip home, leaving the kids to rejoice in victory, while you spend the next 40 to 50 years of your life without a mate.

8. Beware of Mom and Dad

Don't take your parents' advice when picking a companion. Accept advice from anyone else you feel you can trust, but beware of any opinions Mom and Dad might have on this topic. Why?

(a) Do you remember how impossible it was during your teens and 20s to find a potential mate who was good enough for Mom? (Or Dad may have been the problem.)
(b) Does having grandchildren to visit them in their old age seem more important to your parents than your happiness?
(c) Does Dad or Mom expect you to consider what his or her friends think about your unmarried status when you are planning out your life?
(d) If you have not pleased either or both of your parents up until now, what makes you think you ever will?

Most parents have the very best of intentions, but don't fight nature when it comes to them. Listen to them respectfully, tell them what they want to hear, and then do what you feel is best for you.

9. Beware of Misperceptions

While engaged in the game of romance, almost everyone will form misperceptions and will be deceived. While you are using Perceptions and Deceptions to lure a companion, your potential companions will certainly be using them to lure you, as well. To suggest that you can avoid falling into this trap would be deceptive on my part. Just try to avoid being too easily tricked and too greatly surprised when it happens. It's easy to be fooled, especially when you're properly charmed in a romantic spell. If you constantly consider this danger, you will be less likely to be blinded and to make hasty decisions. Remember, though, that it is easy to fool yourself. We somehow develop many common misperceptions all on our own about life with a spouse. For example:

a. Men always think their wives WILL NOT CHANGE after they get married and are almost always surprised. Most women become a bit less sweet, considerate, attentive, obliging, and charming after the honeymoon ends.
b. Women always think their husbands WILL CHANGE after they get married and are almost always surprised. Most men remain just as sloppy, ill-mannered, inconsiderate, neglectful, and selfish after the knot is tied as they were before.

So what can you do to avoid major misperceptions? Probably nothing. But it helps to ask yourself WHY several times when making decisions. Then you pick an entry and lay your money down like the rest of us gamblers.

10. Have Fun

If dating sounds like dirty work, then you need to work on your attitude. Finding a companion should be an exciting, enjoyable adventure. Keeping a sense of humor, putting a glow on your face, developing a good, warm attitude, and generating enthusiasm will definitely help. As you successfully carry out parts of your plan, reward yourself with a special treat. If you cannot approach dating with zest and vibrance, either you have the wrong plan or you don't need a companion. If you laugh and have fun, your chances for success will rapidly escalate.

SUMMARY

ALL JOKES ASIDE, HOW WELL HAVE YOU READ BETWEEN THE LINES?

The following outline summarizes the main points of Chapters 1 through 8. Use it as a reference when developing your best-known methods for finding a companion.

A. Reflect on your life to date.
1. Goals achieved?
2. Goals unfulfilled?
3. New goals?
4. Barriers to unfulfilled goals?
5. Reasons to be optimistic?

B. Review and list personal objectives.

C. Review alternatives.
1. List alternatives for meeting each objective.
2. Pinpoint which objectives can best be fulfilled by acquiring a companion.
3. Ask yourself, "Is a companion the right solution for me?"

4. Establish proof of the need for a companion.

D. Do an honest and thorough self-assessment.
1. Your personality?
2. Your physical appearance, hygiene, and sex appeal?
3. Your communication skills and body language?
4. Your preferences and primary values?
5. Your self-concept/self-worth?
6. Your relationships with others?
7. Your concept of friendship and love?
8. Your lifestyle, habits, and tendencies?
9. Characteristics of your parents and others like you?

E. List your weaknesses and assets.

F. Assess how others perceive you.
1. Initial perceptions of you by others?
2. Lasting perceptions of you by long-time acquaintances?
3. Misconceptions of you by others?
4. Reasons for misconceptions?

G. Evaluate your situation.
1. Strengths you want to keep? How?
2. Weaknesses you want to eliminate or turn into strengths? How?

H. List criteria you want to use in selecting a companion.
1. Ideal list of all desired criteria?
2. Ask "Why" several times to determine the criteria that you must keep.
3. Realistic list of vital few criteria?

I. Develop your plan for getting a companion that meets your criteria.
1. Identify places and situations where you can meet plenty of potential companions.
2. Get yourself there at the right time and make contact.
3. Get their attention and present your best side.
4. Use your realistic list of selection criteria to evaluate the candidates.
5. If a candidate appears to be a winner, begin to establish a relationship.
6. Continue to present your assets and to examine those of the potential companion.
7. When you are convinced you have a winner, move toward a permanent relationship.

J. Execute your plan and continually improve it.
1. Load your calendar with activities in your plan.
2. Create an image that is pleasant, attractive, cheerful, warm, and problem-free.
3. Avoid too much deception.
4. Avoid being deterred by unrealistic fear and pride.
5. Practice the approach until you become comfortable, confident, and proficient.
6. Incorporate new and improved methods for success as you discover them.
7. Execute with steady and unrelenting discipline.
8. Engage the help of others.
9. When in need of rest and/or protection, retreat temporarily and then continue toward your goal. Be determined.
10. Use all of your senses to stay aware of things going on around you. Make good use of your listening skills.

K. Remember these extra tips.
1. Be optimistic.
2. Be active in a relationship with someone.

3. Be patient, calm, cool, and collected.
4. Maintain your health, dignity, and self-respect.
5. Be aware of the dangers and confusions associated with sex.
6. Learn from your mistakes; consider them opportunities for more success.
7. Make sure you and your potential companion succeed with any kids involved.
8. When taking advice about finding a companion from people who have a stake in your decision (like Mom and Dad), be sure your choice is best for you.
9. Use good judgment when accepting perceived characteristics of potential companions. Ask WHY several times to test what you have perceived.
10. Make the venture FUN by keeping a sense of humor, smiling often, developing a good attitude, and being enthusiastic. Reward yourself for good discipline and for small successes.

In closing, let me remind you that to succeed at anything you need a goal, the desire, and a plan; by now, you should have enough ideas to formulate a plan with best-known methods for success. Now you know that you have a choice of companions, that plenty of opportunities await you, and that success depends solely upon you. So plan, practice, and execute, and at the same time relax, laugh, learn, and succeed. There is no reason why the best that life has to offer can't be yours.

BIBLIOGRAPHY

*S*ome readers will want more detailed instruction in specific areas of interest. The following books should offer you additional ideas for less stress and more success in finding a good companion.

A. ASSESSMENT AND GOAL SETTING
- Robert F. Mager, *Goal Analysis*. Belmont, California: David S. Lake Publishers, 1984.
- Sonya Friedman, *On A Clear Day You Can See Yourself*. Boston: Little, Brown and Company, 1991.

B. MOTIVATION AND SELF-WORTH
- Virginia Satir, *Peoplemaking*. Palo Alto, California: Science and Behavior Books, 1972.
- Aubrey C. Daniels & Theodore A. Rosen, *Performance Management*. Tucker, Georgia: Performance Management Publications, 1987.

C. PROBLEM SOLVING AND IMPROVEMENT
- William Glasser, *Control Theory (Take Effective Control Of Your Life)*. New York: Harper & Row, 1984.
- Roger von Oech, *A Whack On The Side Of The Head*. New York: Warner Books, 1983.

- Lorne C. Plunkett & Guy A. Hale, *The Proactive Manager (The Complete Book of Problem Solving and Decision Making)*. New York: John Wiley & Sons, 1982.

D. RELATIONSHIPS
- Leo Buscaglia, *Loving Each Other (The Challenge Of Human Relationships)*. Thorofare, New Jersey: Slack, 1984.
- Gerald W. Piaget & Barbara Binkley, *How To Communicate Under Pressure (Dealing Effectively With Difficult People)*. Portola Valley, California: IAHB Press, 1982.
- Lyman K. Steil, *Listening, It Can Change Your Life*. New York: John Wiley & Sons, 1983.

E. SELECTION, PLANNING, AND DECISION MAKING
- Charles H. Kepner & Benjamin B. Tregoe, *The New Rational Manager*. Princeton, New Jersey: Princeton Research Press, 1981.
- Kenneth Blanchard & Spencer Johnson, *The One Minute Manager*. New York: William Morrow Co., 1981.

F. ACHIEVING SUCCESS
- Dale Carnegie, *How To Win Friends And Influence People*. New York: Simon and Schuster, 1981.
- M. Scott Peck, *The Road Less Traveled*. New York: Simon and Schuster, 1978.
- Denis Waitley, *Ten Seeds Of Greatness*. Old Tappan, New Jersey: Fleming H. Revell Company, 1981.

ABOUT THE AUTHOR

J. Michael Lewis, the happily married father of four adolescent girls, is a recognized expert in creative problem solving. His M.S. in Human Resources Engineering complements twenty years of experience in industry and private consulting. Lewis specializes in finding and applying available principles and techniques in various fields of human endeavor to achieve high performance and excellence. He has successfully taught his methods to audiences ranging from managers, scientists, businessmen, and educators to children, the common denominator being their pursuit of ambitious goals.

Lewis excels at gathering the best-known methods of experts in a particular field, condensing them into the essential elements needed for success, and presenting this information as an easily understood and workable plan to reach a desired goal. Because the published methods included in his plans for success often seem too overwhelming and confusing for everyday, practical use, Lewis adds value to the best-known methods of experts by making them accessible to the lay audience.

An additional key to Lewis' growing popularity is his light-hearted style: he believes that people can learn and relate more effectively when they can relax, reflect, and laugh. His abundant paradoxes and comical illustrations, which create lasting images of important details, reduce his audience's stress. The

www.ingramcontent.com/pod-product-compliance
Lightning Source LLC
Chambersburg PA
CBHW030533080526
44586CB00011B/420